6/88

Ancient Greeks /
J 938 HOR   221263

Horton, Casey.

Date Due

NOV 18 '9			
APR 03 '97			
MAY 29 '97			
FEB 18 '99			
SEP 16 04			
AR 20 08			

J
938   3730
Horton, Casey
Ancient Greeks

OVERSIZE

LONGLAC PUBLIC LIBRA

D1377285

Ancient Greeks

CONTENTS

© Aladdin Books Ltd

Designed and produced by
Aladdin Books Ltd
70 Old Compton Street
London W1

All rights reserved

Printed in Belgium

First published in the
United States in 1984 by
Gloucester Press
387 Park Avenue South
New York NY 10016

ISBN 0-531-03484-4

Library of Congress
Catalog Card No. 84-81107

Certain illustrations have previously appeared in the "Civilization Library"
series published by Gloucester Press

THE CIVILIZATION LIBRARY

Ancient Greeks

CASEY HORTON

Illustrated by

IVAN LAPPER

Consultant

HAMISH DUNCAN

Gloucester Press
New York · Toronto · 1984

The coming of the Greeks

The land that we call ancient Greece was made up of many islands in the Aegean Sea, and land on either side of it. Before 2000 B.C. (Before Christ), most of this area was occupied by people who did not speak the Greek language.

The first Greek speaking people to arrive in this part of the world were invaders who came from the north. They came in gradually, but the most important invasions happened just before 2000 B.C. These settlers built fortresses at Mycenae and in other parts of the country to defend themselves from other invaders.

Mycenae was the center of the first civilization on the continent of Europe. It lasted from 4000 until 1100 B.C. In the Dark ages that followed (1100-700 B.C.), the writing and art of the Mycenaeans disappeared.

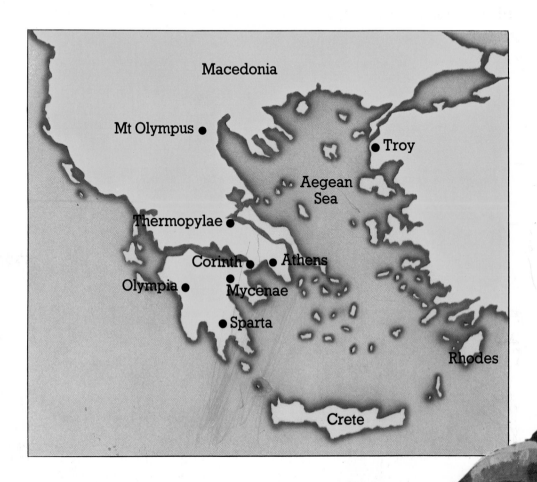

Macedonia

Mt Olympus

Troy

Aegean
Sea

Thermopylae

Corinth   Athens

Olympia   Mycenae

Sparta

Rhodes

Crete

The story of Troy

The Greeks had many legends, and one of these told how the Mycenaeans attacked the city of Troy in Asia Minor. Helen, the wife of Menelaus, was taken to the city of Troy by a Trojan called Paris. The king of Mycenae, Agamemnon, went to Troy with an army to avenge themselves on the Trojans.

The long war

Many Greek heroes went with Agamemnon, including Achilles, Odysseus and Ajax. The war that followed lasted for ten years. Achilles, the greatest of the Greek heroes, was killed; so was Hector, the hero of Troy. In the tenth year the Greeks, who were camped near Troy, pretended to retreat. Before the city gates they left a huge wooden horse. The Trojans wheeled the horse into the city. Late at night Greek soldiers, who had hidden inside it, set fire to Troy. They then let the rest of the army inside and the city was destroyed.

The battle for Troy

5

A simple life

Most of the ancient Greeks were farmers. They farmed on hillsides and small plains. On the plains they used oxen to pull the plows and prepare the ground for sowing. They grew vegetables such as peas and beans and cereals such as barley. On the hillsides they grew olive trees and grapevines.

As well as growing crops, most farmers kept some animals. Herds of sheep and goats grazed on rocky hillsides. Pigs were allowed to roam through the woods to feed on acorns.

Life on the land was very hard, especially during the harvest. Then, all the family worked from early morning to dusk to cut and store the grain.

A Greek farmer plows the land.

Living off the land

The farmer and his family used almost everything on the land for food and clothing. Bread made from barley was the main food. The sheep and goats gave milk, and their skins and wool were used to make clothes. The Greeks did not often kill animals for meat, but sometimes a young lamb was killed and eaten in spring. People who lived near the sea ate fish and other seafood. Most of the food was cooked in olive oil. Grapes were either eaten as fruit or made into wine. Apples, nuts and honey were also part of the Greeks' diet. If farmers had more grain or wine than they could use, they traded it for things they could not make themselves.

The Greeks frowned on gluttony, and most people ate only two meals a day, a light "brunch" in the late morning – perhaps only bread, cheese and olives washed down with water – and a more substantial evening meal. The very poor lived on barley (as bread or porridge), garlic, onions and not much else.

Above: Main foods in the Greek diet.

The City of Athens

Athens was one of the most important cities in ancient Greece. Like other great cities in Greece it had once been just a place where people met to trade. Gradually, more and more people began to live there and many splendid buildings were built. There were fine temples, public squares and buildings with many columns and open spaces. The streets and buildings were planned carefully and laid out in an orderly way. Above the city was the Acropolis – the "high city" – with the temple called the Parthenon. Ruins of the Acropolis can still be seen today.

The Athenian house

Most of the houses in Athens were built around an open courtyard. The Greeks liked to spend as much time as possible in the fresh air. The rooms for living in led off this open area. Sleeping quarters were placed in the upper part of the house. Greek houses had several things that we think of as modern. For example, they had drains to take away waste water, and wells or fountains in the courtyard for fresh water.

An Athenian house

The city of Athens at the height of its splendor. The Acropolis is set on top of the rock.

Colonies and trade

As the number of people in Greece grew, there was not enough land or food for everyone. At the beginning of the 8th century B.C. many people were sent away to start new colonies. Colonies were founded in Northern Greece, the Black Sea, in Italy, Sicily and North Africa. In these new settlements the people farmed the land, just as others still did at home. Once the settlers were organized they could trade their extra grain with cities such as Athens and Corinth. These cities sent pottery and other goods to the colonies.

The ships that carried these items sailed from April until September. The Greek sailors did not have compasses. They steered their ships by watching landmarks, and at night they steered by following the stars.

Early Greeks used iron rods or spits for trading. Later, coins called drachmas were used.

A trading ship unloads pottery in the port of a Greek colony.

11

The home of democracy

The ancient Greeks developed the idea of democracy, which they called *demokratia* – "rule of the people." This meant that every male citizen could speak in the Assembly and decide how the city was run. The Assembly was kept in order by a special group called the Council of 500. Each of the 10 divisions of Athens, the "tribes," named candidates for the Assembly. These men drew lots to determine which of them would sit on the Council. Each tribe also elected a warrior for the Board of Ten Generals. The generals led the armies and defended Athens from its enemies.

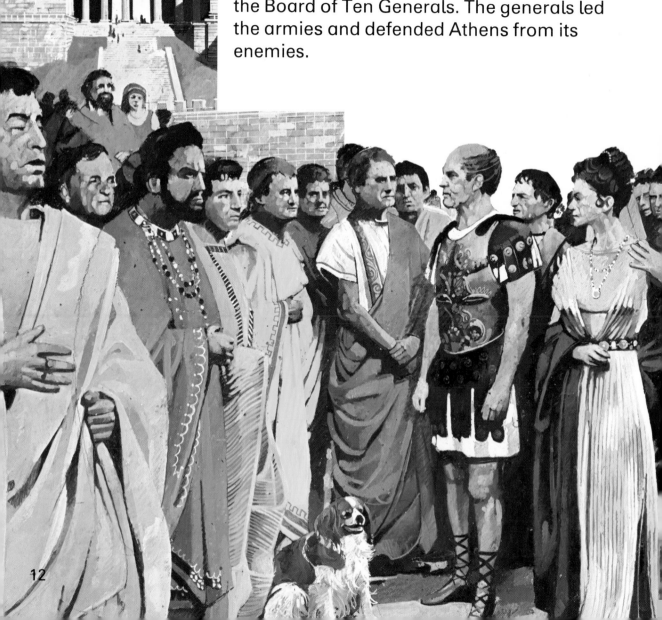

Generals and heroes

In the 5th century B.C. the generals became the real leaders of Athens. Yet they still had to answer to the citizens for their mistakes. During this period the Athenians developed a large empire in the Aegean. The most famous of Athens' great leaders came from the Board of Generals. His name was Pericles, and even today he is still thought of as a great man. Pericles was admired for his stirring speeches, his honesty and his thinking. He was responsible for many of Athens' great buildings and he helped to build the Athenian Empire. However, this popular man led Athens into war with the city of Sparta. Called the Peloponnesian War, it lasted for 27 years and led to the ruin of Athens.

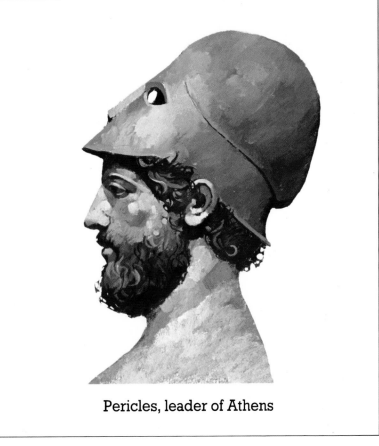

Pericles, leader of Athens

Life in the open air

The climate in Greece was very pleasant. It encouraged the people to spend much of their time in the fresh air. The streets of Athens were lined with elegant public buildings. Here male citizens could be entertained, play a sport or follow the favorite Greek pastime – talking to their friends. There were bath houses, wrestling schools, a singing hall, a market, theaters, numerous temples, law courts, and a large hall where the council met.

The theater was in the open air. On the circular stage, actors played both male and female roles. They wore elaborate masks to identify the characters they were playing. Comedies often attacked important public figures and made them look ridiculous. Tragedies were usually retellings of ancient myths.

LONGLAC PUBLIC LIBRARY

Festivals and banquets

Religious festivals were very important events in the Greek year. These were held to honor a god, such as Dionysus, the god of wine, or Athena, the goddess of wisdom and purity. At ceremonies and festivals women had a chance to appear in public. In Athens, girls from wealthy families took part in a procession to the Acropolis to change the robes of Athena. They were accompanied by chariots, wealthy men and musicians.

Only wealthy men attended banquets, where they feasted and drank wine diluted with water. Female musicians and dancers entertained. They were usually slaves or women who were considered to be of a lower class than wives and daughters.

A Spartan life

Life in Sparta was very different from life in Athens. There was no democracy here; the city was ruled by two kings, a Council of Elders and an Assembly. From the age of seven, young boys were trained to fight and obey orders. Those fit to be warriors were sent away from home. They had hard, physical training and served the adult soldiers. When they were 20 years old they joined a military squad, as part of Sparta's fighting force. Spartans were among the best fighters in Greece.

Contrasts in lifestyles

Spartan boys spent years in grim barracks.

Athenian children enjoyed a warm family life.

Self-sufficiency was encouraged in Spartans.

Thought and communication counted for more in Athens.

The "Equals"

Young men remained in military camps until they were 30 years old. After that they were part of the reserve army and fought for their people when necessary. For this reason, the women of Sparta were freer than Athenian women. While the men were away they ran the farms and ruled the household. Spartan girls were given athletic training so they would grow up to be strong and healthy. In theory, all Spartans were equal in government and war.

Sinister and tough, Spartan soldiers had one small indulgence – they wore their hair long, and always perfumed it before battle.

Pictures from a Greek vase.

18

In honor of the gods

LONGLAC PUBLIC LIBRARY

The early Greeks held sporting contests during their religious festivals. From these came the special "games," where competitors vied with each other for the honor of winning. Beginning in 775 B.C. the games were held every four years at Olympia. Contestants offered sacrifices to the gods before the start. They also took an oath to play by the rules.

Fair play

The favorite sport was running, and there was a race for athletes wearing armor. Other events included jumping, throwing the javelin and discus, and wrestling. Wrestling could be very fierce and sometimes included strangling and kicking. The only event for teams was chariot racing. Only free Greeks were allowed to compete – slaves could not enter the games.

Art, thought and belief

During the late 5th and 4th centuries B.C. Athens produced three playwrights whose works are still performed today: Aeschylus, author of *Agamemnon*; Sophocles, author of the great tragedies *Antigone* and *Oedipus the King*; and Euripides, who wrote *Medea*. Another great writer of the period was Herodotus, the first important writer of history, now known as the "Father of History." Homer, the poet who wrote about the siege of Troy in the *Iliad* lived much earlier. The great philosophers of this time included Socrates, Plato and Aristotle, the teacher of Alexander the Great. In Greece, *philosophia* meant "love of wisdom." We think of philosophy as the study of man in his world. To the Greeks it also meant the study of science.

Writers and philosophers

The gods of Olympus

The Greeks believed in gods and goddesses, whom they said made their home on Mount Olympus. Of these, there were 12 who were above all the others, including Zeus, the god of the heavens, Poseidon, god of the sea, and Zeus' wife Hera, protector of marriage.

The Greeks believed that the gods looked and acted like humans, but were superior to humans in many ways. For example, gods did not grow older and they did not die. They also had enormous powers which they could use to help humans, or, if they were angry, make things difficult for them. Greeks prayed to the gods and made sacrifices to them to ask for help.

A selection of gods and goddesses taken from Greek vases.

The scientists

The world and its people were of great interest to the Greeks. They observed, gathered information and explained what they saw. Pythagoras, a mathematician of the 6th century B.C., found many relationships between numbers. For example, he discovered that 10 is the sum of its first four integers: 1+2+3+4=10. These numbers and their sum made a pattern – a *tetraktys*, or triangle. In the same way, he showed that nine is the sum of successive odd numbers (1+3+5) and becomes a square when it is laid out with counters. He or one of his students, also discovered that the length of a string on an instrument was related to the pitch of the notes in the musical scale. When a string, marked from 1 to 12, is plucked at points 6, 8, 9 and 12, it gives the descending scale (do, so, fa, do). When the string is halved, the two dos are exactly an octave apart.

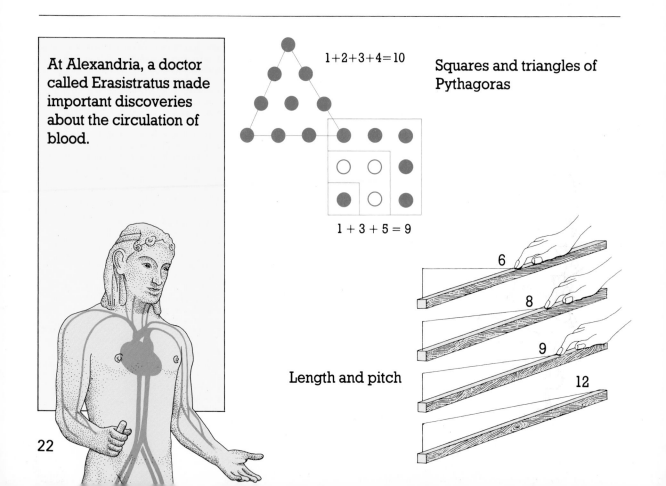

At Alexandria, a doctor called Erasistratus made important discoveries about the circulation of blood.

1+2+3+4=10

Squares and triangles of Pythagoras

1 + 3 + 5 = 9

Length and pitch

6

8

9

12

An early kind of clock

Greek scientists knew how to measure time. In Athens, beneath the Acropolis, a clock was built in a tower called the Tower of the Winds. The clock was driven by water power. From a spring, water filled a reservoir. The water then flowed through a pipe into a tank with a float in it. Water dripping into the tank raised the float which raised a chain. The chain ran through pulleys to a sandbag counterweight. As it was let down, the counterweight turned the clock disk. The tank was drained every 24 hours and this reset the clock. A pointer on the side of the tower measured the seasons.

The tradition of Greek scientific thought was pioneered by one of the most famous philosophers, Aristotle, best known for his work on physics and logic. It influenced European science until the 17th century.

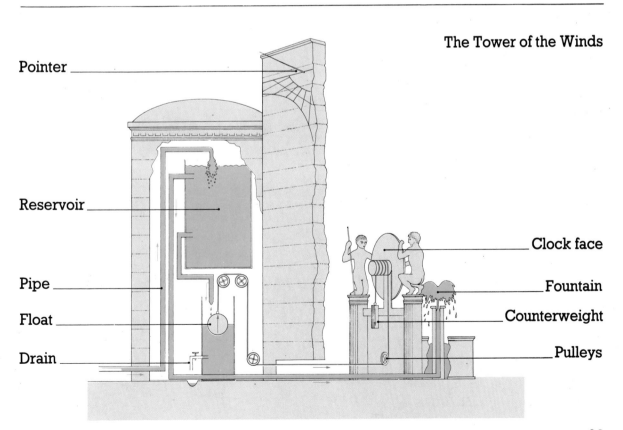

The Tower of the Winds

Pointer

Reservoir

Pipe

Float

Drain

Clock face

Fountain

Counterweight

Pulleys

Battle with the Persians

Soon after 550 B.C. the Persian king, Cyrus, took control of Greek lands on the Aegean east coast. This Persian territory gradually grew to the north. Eventually the Greeks under Persian rule revolted. They asked the free Greeks to help them. But it was not until a new king, Xerxes, decided to win all of Greece that the Greeks really came into battle with the Persians.

By then, many of the Greeks had surrendered. However, the Athenians and Spartans and some other smaller states agreed to face the Persians. They elected Sparta as the leader on land and sea. Both the Greek army and navy were about half the size of those belonging to the Persians. Xerxes had scoured his huge empire for the soldiers and ships of many nations.

In the face of defeat

The Spartans made a stand in a narrow pass at Thermopylae in central Greece in 480 B.C. They fought bravely, but in the end the Persians defeated them. All the Spartans were killed, and the way was clear. Xerxes and his fighting force made for Athens.

In Athens, the Greek soldiers took to the sea. At Salamis, an island near Athens, Persians and Greeks met in a narrow channel. The Persian fleet split up to encircle Salamis, perhaps to try and take the Greek navy from the rear. The plan did not work. As Xerxes' main fleet entered a narrow channel, the Greeks emerged from small inlets and fell upon it. The Persians had very fast boats, but the heavier Athenian boats were better suited to the battle. As more and more Persian ships poured into the channel they found themselves caught up in the chaos. The crews panicked and began to retreat.

Xerxes watched the fighting from a hill. He lost 200 of his ships, but the Athenians lost only 40. A year later, in 479 B.C., the Greeks also defeated the Persian army in central Greece.

Encounter at Salamis

Greek against Greek

After the naval battle at Salamis the Athenian navy became very powerful. Although the Spartans had a fine army they were afraid that Athens would use its navy to take over Spartan territory. In the end this led Sparta to attack Athens.

The first part of the war between Sparta and Athens (the Peloponnesian War) lasted for ten years – from 431 to 421 B.C. Finally both sides were exhausted by the fighting and agreed to peace. However, when Athens tried to conquer the distant island of Sicily, they failed. The soldiers suffered from disease and bad leadership and were defeated by their enemies. In 413 B.C. Sparta began the Peloponnesian War again. Because the Athenians were weak Sparta defeated them in 404 B.C.

Armor of a warrior

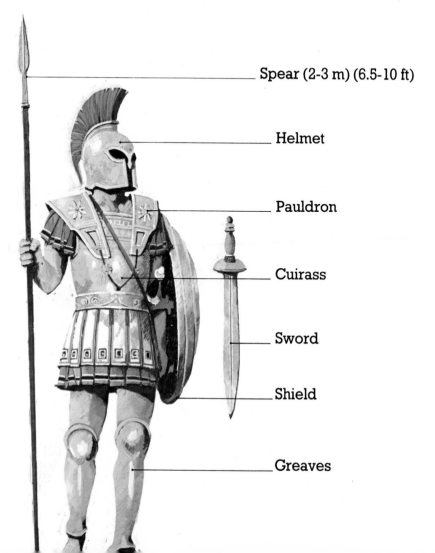

Spear (2-3 m) (6.5-10 ft)

Helmet

Pauldron

Cuirass

Sword

Shield

Greaves

A strategy for killing

The heavily armored foot soldiers in the Greek armies were called *hoplites*. A group of these men made up the *phalanx*. When they formed up for battle, each hoplite was partly protected by the shield of the hoplite standing next to him.

During a battle, the hoplites made the main attack on the enemy. Other foot soldiers called *peltasts* stood on either side of them, and beyond the peltasts were the cavalry (mounted soldiers). The peltasts attacked first with their spears. Then the hoplites advanced in hand to hand fighting. The peltasts and cavalry made a circle around them and the enemy. If the enemy broke ranks and ran away, the cavalry chased after them.

The *phalanx*

Alexander the Great

Alexander, King of Macedonia, was perhaps the most famous Greek military leader. Soon after he became king in 336 B.C. he invaded Asia Minor, held by the Persians. Alexander had reinforcements sent out from Macedonia to replace the men who were killed. He also left manned fortresses behind him on the route to hold the territory he had gained. Alexander took a great interest in his troops and gained the loyalty of his men. By 330 B.C. he had seized many Persian cities, burnt the capital Persepolis (opposite), and had complete control of the Persian Empire.

Victory and death in the East

Alexander then traveled to the East, as far as present-day India. He thought that if he kept moving eastward he would come to the end of the world. Along the way he established many colonies. Some of them he called Alexandria, after himself. At Taxila, after a great battle, his men refused to go any further. They were tired and many of them were ill. Alexander then turned toward home, and spent the winter of 324-323 B.C. at Babylon. There he caught a fever and died.

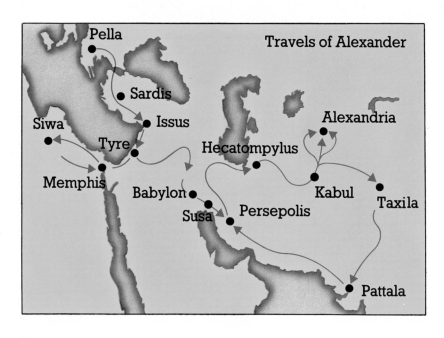

Travels of Alexander

Out of the past

LONGLAC PUBLIC LIBRARY

Today the ruins of the Acropolis stand high above the modern city of Athens. People from all parts of the world still come to visit these and other ruins of the Greek civilization. Greek ruins are not only found in Greece. Some of them still stand in parts of the Mediterranean that once belonged to the Greek Empire. They remind us of the beauty of ancient Greece and the greatness of the Greek people who lived so long ago.

The influence of ancient Greece

The world we live in – Western civilization – owes many things to the ancient Greeks. Many of the words we use were invented by Greeks – words such as democracy, poetry, philosophy and logic.

We have seen how the word democracy stands for an idea, the idea that each person should be able to decide how his or her country should be governed. So we have not only inherited words from the Greeks, we have also inherited ideas and ways of thinking from them.

In the Western world the study of mathematics, science and the world itself began with the Greeks. Even the geometry we are taught at school was invented by the Greek Euclid who lived about 300 B.C. – almost 2300 years ago.

Glossary

Acropolis The hill above Athens which was once used as a fortress to defend the city. One of its most important buildings was the Parthenon, the temple of the goddess Athena.

Colony An independent city settled by people who had left their homeland.

Counterweight A weight that balances another weight.

Civilization A society that has developed writing, arts and science as well as laws and regulations for governing the people.

Dark Ages In Greece, the period between 1100 and 700 B.C. when Greece was cut off from the outside world and the art of writing was not used.

Drachma The silver coin that was the unit of Greek money.

Integer A whole number. That is, any number that is not a fraction.

Legend A story handed down from one generation to another.

Playwright A person who writes plays.

Index